Title: It's All or Nothing
Subtitle: Rethinking Biblical Giving in Light of the Gospel
Written by: Christian A. Dickinson
Illustrations by: Learning Engineered LLC
Published by: Learning Engineered Publishing

Library of Congress Control Number: 2025937920
ISBN (Print): 978-1-965741-16-0

First Edition: 2025

Printed & Created in: United States of America
Text and Illustration Copyright © 2025

Learning Engineered Publishing is a division of Learning Engineered LLC and a subsidiary of Carpe Diem Unlimited Holdings, Inc.

LEARNING ENGINEERED
PUBLISHING

Contents

Preface

G rowing up, I never heard, **"Give God 10% and He'll bless the rest."**
My family didn't sit down with a calculator to figure out what we owed God. Instead, our home was a living example of radical generosity—no percentages, no rules, just open hands.

We didn't belong to a traditional church with pews or offering plates. Our "church" was our living room, where my dad and a few others taught the Bible. There were no budgets or tithing campaigns, but our door was always open. Missionaries stayed with us for weeks—sometimes months—eating at our table without a bill. My parents gave away cars, paid for travel, or handed over cash when they saw a need. My dad would say, **"Everything we have is God's to give or take."**

This wasn't about wealth—we weren't rich. It was about trust. A single mom might join us for dinner, or a struggling family might get a bag of groceries. Giving wasn't a transaction—it was worship, like singing a hymn or praying. It flowed from love, not obligation.

Later, when I joined other churches, I was surprised to hear tithing preached as a must-do—often tied to blessings or guilt. It didn't match the freedom I'd seen at home. That tension sparked this book.

Is tithing really what God asks of us? Or does Jesus call us to something bigger—giving not just a portion, but all of who we are?

Whether you're in a megachurch or a house church, rich or barely getting by, this book is for you. We'll explore what the Bible says about generosity—from the Old Testament to the New—and why Jesus' way is about your heart, not a number.

Ready to rethink giving? Let's uncover the roots of tithing and see where God's Spirit leads us.

Introduction: It's All or Nothing

Picture a young man kneeling before Jesus, asking, **"What must I do to inherit eternal life?"**
He's kept every rule, but Jesus looks at him and says, **"Sell everything, give to the poor, and follow me"** *(Mark 10:21)*. Not 10%. Everything.

That's the heart of this book.

Tithing—giving 10%—is a cornerstone in many churches. You've probably heard it: **"Give God your first 10%, and He'll bless the rest."** It's taught as obedience, a key to God's favor. But what if Jesus has something bigger in mind?

The Old Testament tied tithing to Israel's laws and temple system. Yet in the New Testament, Jesus and Paul never command it. Instead, they call for radical generosity—giving that flows from trust, not a calculator.

Growing up in a home church, I saw this first-hand: my parents gave freely, not because of a percentage, but because God led them. Whether it was a meal for a stranger or money for a missionary, their giving was worship—not a rule.

Maybe you've only known tithing as a church requirement. That's okay. This book invites you to ask:

What does God really want from my giving?

We'll explore:

- The roots of tithing in Israel's covenant (**Chapter 1**).

- What Jesus taught about giving (**Chapter 2**).

- Paul's vision of generosity (**Chapter 3**).

- Why tithing arguments don't hold up

(**Chapter 4**).

- The heart of New Testament giving and how to live it (**Chapters 5–6**).

- Why churches cling to tithing and how to break free (**Chapter 7**).

This isn't just about theology—it's about living with open hands, whether you have a lot or a little. Jesus isn't asking for 10%. **He's asking for everything.**

Let's dive into the Bible's story of giving—starting with where tithing began.

Chapter 1

The Origins of Tithing

Imagine giving not because you have to, but because your heart overflows with gratitude. That's how tithing started—not as a rule, but as a response to God's goodness. Many think tithing—giving 10%—is God's timeless standard for every believer. But the Bible tells a different story, rooted in ancient Israel's covenant, not today's church.

Let's trace tithing's origins to see why it's not about a percentage—it's about everything.

The First Mentions of Tithing

Picture Abram, fresh from a battle victory, standing before Melchizedek, a priest-king of God Most High. Out of a grateful heart, he of-

fers a tenth of his spoils—not because God demanded it, but because he wanted to honor the
One who saved him. **Then Abram gave him a
tenth of everything. — Genesis 14:20**

This wasn't a law or a habit—it was a one-time
act of worship. Later, Jacob, awestruck by a
dream of God's promise at Bethel, makes a
vow: **"...and of all that you give me I will give
you a tenth." — Genesis 28:22**

He ties his giving to God's protection: **"If God
will be with me... then the Lord will be my
God." — Genesis 28:20–21**

This wasn't a command—it was a personal
pledge, like a song of trust. These early gifts
show giving as an overflow of faith, not a check-
list. That changes how we think about generosity today.

These voluntary acts set the stage for Israel's
structured tithing system.

The Law of Tithing in Israel

Under Moses, tithing became a system, but it wasn't a simple 10% to a church. Israel's tithes were complex, tied to their covenant with God:

- **Levitical Tithe**: A tenth of crops and livestock supported the landless Levites, like a religious tax (Numbers 18:21–24).

- **Festival Tithe**: Another tenth funded feasts to worship together (Deuteronomy 14:22–27).

- **Welfare Tithe**: Every third year, a tenth helped orphans, widows, and foreigners (Deuteronomy 14:28–29).

Together, these added up to 23–30% a year—a national economic system, not a personal spiritual act. Whether you were a wealthy farmer or a struggling herder, these tithes were about Israel's covenant, not your heart's devotion.

But was tithing about money? Not at all.

Was Tithing About Money?

Tithing was agricultural, rooted in Israel's land-based economy: **"Be sure to set aside a tenth of all that your fields produce each year." — Deuteronomy 14:22**

Grain, wine, oil, livestock—that's what God asked for, not coins or paychecks. This specificity shows tithing was for Israel's time and place, not a universal rule for all believers.

What About Malachi 3:10?

Many quote this verse to urge tithing: **"Bring the whole tithe into the storehouse, that there may be food in my house. Test me in this," says the Lord Almighty, "and see if I will not... pour out so much blessing..." — Malachi 3:10**

But picture Malachi confronting priests who hoarded grain while Levites and the poor starved. The "storehouse" was a temple room for food, not a church bank account. This was about Israel's covenant faithfulness, not a promise of wealth for Christians today.

Tithing's roots lead us to a bigger question: Does it still apply?

The Transition to the New Testament

Tithing was tied to:

- The Levitical priesthood, now obsolete (**Hebrews 7:12**).

- The temple was destroyed in AD 70.

- Israel's agrarian economy, not our modern world.

Without a New Testament command to tithe, Jesus offers something radical: Spirit-led generosity, giving not just 10%, but everything.

Key Takeaways

- Tithing began as voluntary worship, not a command (Abram and Jacob).

- Israel's tithes were a national system, totaling 23–30%, not a spiritual act.

- Tithing was agricultural, not about money or paychecks.

- Malachi 3:10 was for Israel's priests, not today's church.

- Tithing is tied to an obsolete covenant, replaced by Jesus' call to total surrender.

Where Do We Go From Here?

Tithing was Israel's system, but Jesus calls us to something bigger—a life of open-handed generosity. Ready to see how He redefined giving? Let's dive into His words next.

Chapter 2
What Did Jesus Say About Tithing?

If tithing were God's plan for us, wouldn't Jesus have said so? He talked a lot about money and giving, but His words point to something deeper—a call to give everything, not just a percentage. Picture a widow giving her last coins or a rich man facing a tough choice. Jesus' teaching isn't about rules—it's about your heart. Let's see how He redefined generosity.

Jesus' Only Direct Mention of Tithing

Jesus mentions tithing once, rebuking the Pharisees: **"Woe to you... Pharisees, you hypocrites! You give a tenth of your spices—mint, dill, and cumin. But you have neglected the more important matters of the law—justice, mercy, and faithfulness.**

You should have practiced the latter, without neglecting the former." — Matthew 23:23

At first glance, this sounds like Jesus endorses tithing. But picture Him speaking to religious leaders still under the Old Covenant, obsessed with tiny details like tithing herbs while ignoring love and justice. He wasn't commanding tithing for us—He was calling out their hypocrisy. His point? Outward acts mean nothing without a heart of faith.

Jesus' real call to giving goes way beyond 10%.

Jesus and the Rich Young Ruler: A Higher Standard

Imagine a wealthy young man kneeling before Jesus, asking, "What must I do to inherit eternal life?" Jesus looks at him with love and says: **"Go, sell everything you have and give to the poor, and you will have treasure in heaven. Then come, follow me." — Mark 10:21**

No 10% here. Jesus asked for everything. This wasn't just about money—it was about where the man's trust lay. For Jesus, generosity isn't a percentage—it's a posture of surrender, whether you're rich or poor.

Jesus Praises the Widow's Offering

Picture Jesus sitting in the temple, watching people drop offerings into the treasury. A poor widow shuffles up, slipping in two small coins—her entire livelihood. **"Truly I tell you, this poor widow has put more into the treasury than all the others. They all gave out of their wealth; but she, out of her poverty, put in everything—all she had to live on." — Mark 12:43–44**

Jesus didn't praise her percentage—He celebrated her trust. Her gift was worship, like a song of faith, showing that in God's Kingdom, it's not about how much you give, but how much you trust.

Jesus' Teaching on Treasure and Trust

Jesus says: **"Do not store up for yourselves treasures on earth... But store up for yourselves treasures in heaven... For where your treasure is, there your heart will be also."** — Matthew 6:19–21

Giving is worship, like praying or serving, anchoring your heart in heaven. He adds: **"Seek first His kingdom and His righteousness, and all these things will be given to you as well."** — Matthew 6:33

Generosity isn't just about money—it's about trusting God above all else, whether you're giving a dollar or a fortune.

Jesus and the Early Church Model

The early church took Jesus' words to heart: **"All the believers were together and had everything in common. They sold property and possessions to give to anyone who had need."** — Acts 2:44–45

No percentages, no rules—just love in action. A family might sell land to feed the hungry. A widow might share her home. This wasn't forced—it was the Spirit moving them to give everything, like Jesus did. Their giving was worship, a reflection of His lordship over all they had.

What Jesus Didn't Say

Jesus never:

- Commanded a tithe.

- Collected a tithe.

- Promised wealth for tithing.

Instead, He called for sacrificial love, trust, and total surrender—a generosity that flows from the heart, not a calculator.

Key Takeaways

- **Jesus rebuked tithing hypocrisy, not endorsed it** (Matthew 23:23).

- **He called for everything, not a percentage** (Mark 10:21).

- **He praised sacrificial trust, like the widow's offering** (Mark 12:44).

- **Giving is worship, anchoring your heart in heaven** (Matthew 6:19–21).

- **The early church gave freely, led by love, not law** (Acts 2:44–45).

Where Do We Go From Here?

Jesus didn't teach tithing—He taught surrender. But how did His followers live this out? Let's see how Paul built on this call to radical generosity.

Chapter 3
What Paul Actually Taught About Giving

If tithing were required, Paul—the guy who wrote half the New Testament—would've told us. But he doesn't. Instead, he paints a picture of giving that's free, joyful, and led by the Spirit. Picture a poor church begging to help others, not because they had to, but because love drove them. Let's see what Paul really taught about generosity.

No Command to Tithe

Paul talks a lot about money and giving, but never once commands tithing. That silence speaks volumes. As the architect of Christian doctrine, he could've mandated 10%, but instead, he points to a better way—giving from the heart, not a rulebook.

What does that heart-driven giving look like?

The Heart of Giving: 2 Corinthians 9

Picture a Macedonian church, scraping by, yet begging to give to others in need: **"They gave as much as they were able, and even beyond their ability… entirely on their own." — 2 Corinthians 8:3–4**

Paul says: **"Whoever sows generously will also reap generously. Each of you should give what you have decided in your heart to give, not reluctantly or under compulsion, for God loves a cheerful giver." — 2 Corinthians 9:6–7**

This isn't a formula—it's a promise of joy. Whether it's a widow giving her time or a merchant sharing his savings, Paul's principles are clear: **Voluntary:** No mandated 10%. **Joyful:** No pressure or guilt. **Heart-led:** God cares about your motive, not the amount.

This freedom raises the bar to total surrender.

Supporting Ministry: 1 Corinthians 9

Paul affirms that ministers should be supported: **"Those who preach the gospel should receive their living from the gospel." — 1 Corinthians 9:14**

But he draws a parallel to Old Testament priests, not a tithing command. A farmer might give grain, a laborer their skills—each gave what they could. Paul himself chose tentmaking over taking support, showing flexibility, not obligation.

The Early Church Model of Giving

Paul told churches: **"On the first day of every week, each one of you should set aside a sum of money in keeping with your income." — 1 Corinthians 16:2**

This wasn't a tithe—it was practical, based on ability. A poor widow might give a coin, a wealthy trader a larger gift—both trusted God. The early church didn't tithe to a central fund;

they gave to meet real needs, like helping the poor or supporting missionaries. It was love, not law.

Why Paul Didn't Reinforce Tithing

Paul's whole theology is about grace, not rules. Just as he rejected circumcision or dietary laws for believers, he didn't carry over tithing. Instead, he called for: **Free giving** (2 Corinthians 9:7), **Flexible support for ministry** (1 Corinthians 9:14), **Proportional gifts based on ability** (1 Corinthians 16:2)

This isn't a lower standard—it's a higher one, inviting you to give everything, led by the Spirit.

Key Takeaways

- Paul never commands tithing, focusing on grace rather than law.

- Giving is voluntary and joyful, not forced (2 Corinthians 9:7).

- Ministry support is flexible, not a fixed percentage *(1 Corinthians 9:14)*.

- Early Christians gave based on need and ability, not rules *(1 Corinthians 16:2)*.

- Grace frees us to give from love, not obligation.

Where Do We Go From Here?

Paul's vision of giving is all about joy, not law. But why do churches still push tithing? Let's test those arguments against Scripture and see what holds up.

Chapter 4

Common Arguments for Tithing—and Why They Fall Short

L ots of churches teach tithing with good hearts, but good intentions don't always mean biblical truth. Picture a pastor quoting Malachi to urge 10%, not knowing it was about grain, not paychecks. As we've seen in Chapters 1–3, tithing isn't a New Testament command. So, let's test the four big arguments for tithing against Scripture and see why they don't hold up for us today.

Argument #1: "Jesus Affirmed Tithing in Matthew 23:23"

The Claim: Jesus says to the Pharisees: **"You give a tenth of your spices... But you have neglected the more important matters of the law—justice, mercy, and faithfulness.**

You should have practiced the latter, without neglecting the former." — Matthew 23:23 Some say this means tithing is required for Christians.

The Truth: Picture Jesus confronting religious leaders obsessed with tithing herbs while ignoring love. He was speaking to Jews under the Old Covenant, before the cross changed everything. He wasn't endorsing tithing for us—He was calling out hypocrisy. If Jesus wanted us to tithe, He'd have said so clearly, but He never did.

This leads to another popular claim.

Argument #2: "Malachi 3:10 Says We Must Bring the Tithe"

The Claim: "Bring the whole tithe into the storehouse, that there may be food in my house..." — Malachi 3:10 Some say this proves Christians must tithe for blessings.

The Truth: Imagine Malachi rebuking priests for hoarding grain while the poor starved. The "storehouse" was a temple room for food, not a church bank account. Malachi was about Israel's covenant, not your paycheck. If churches followed Malachi, they'd collect crops for the needy, not cash for buildings.

But what about promises of wealth?

Argument #3: "Tithing Ensures Financial Blessing"

The Claim: Some teach that tithing guarantees prosperity—give 10%, and God will multiply your money.

The Truth: No New Testament verse promises wealth for tithing. Paul says give joyfully, not to "get" *(2 Corinthians 9:7)*. Picture faithful Christians like Paul, often poor yet rich in faith. Giving isn't a spiritual investment scheme—it's worship, trusting God whether you're rich or struggling.

One last argument keeps tithing alive.

Argument #4: "Tithing Supports the Church"

The Claim: Without tithing, churches can't pay pastors or run ministries.

The Truth: The early church didn't tithe—they shared freely *(Acts 4:32–35)*. A single mom might give $5, a business owner $500—both support God's work. Paul says ministers should be supported *(1 Corinthians 9:14)*, but not through mandatory tithes. Churches relying on a 10% risk are acting like businesses, not faith communities. Giving should come from love, not pressure.

What Does Scripture Really Teach?

Giving isn't a tax—it's worship, a way to say, "God, I trust You with everything." Scripture shows:

- No tithing command for Christians *(Chapters 2–3)*

- Malachi was for Israel, not the church *(Chapter 1)*

- No prosperity promise for tithing *(2 Corinthians 9:7)*

- Giving is voluntary and joyful, not forced *(Acts 4:32)*

- Church support is biblical, but from the heart, not percentages *(1 Corinthians 9:14)*

Key Takeaways

- Jesus didn't endorse tithing for us—He called out hypocrisy *(Matthew 23:23)*

- Malachi 3:10 was about Israel's priests, not church budgets

- Tithing doesn't guarantee wealth—giving is about worship, not reward

- Early Christians gave freely, not by percentages *(Acts 4:32)*

- Support churches with love, not obligation *(1 Corinthians 9:14)*

Where Do We Go From Here?

Tithing doesn't hold up, but what does giving look like today? Let's explore the heart of New Testament generosity and how to live it out.

Chapter 5

New Testament Giving – A Heart of Generosity

Imagine a widow dropping her last two coins into the temple treasury, trusting God with everything she has. That's the heart of New Testament giving—not a percentage, but a posture of love. Does God expect us to support the church, help the poor, and live generously? Absolutely. But it's about your heart, not a number. Let's see how Jesus and the apostles call us to radical generosity.

1. Giving Is Voluntary, Not Obligatory

New Testament giving isn't a tax—it's a choice. Paul writes: **"Each of you should give what you have decided in your heart to give, not reluctantly or under compulsion, for God loves a cheerful giver." — 2 Corinthians 9:7**

This means: You decide: Pray and choose what to give, led by the Spirit. No pressure: Giving is an invitation to love, not a law. Joy matters: God treasures your heart more than the amount.

Picture a student slipping $5 to a homeless shelter or a family funding a church outreach. It's not about obligation—it's love responding to grace, as Paul taught (Chapter 3). This freedom leads us to give from what we have.

2. Giving Is Proportional to One's Ability

God doesn't demand 10%—He asks for what you can give. **"On the first day of every week, each one of you should set aside a sum of money in keeping with your income." — 1 Corinthians 16:2**

It's about fairness: Those with abundance can give more—maybe funding a missionary. Those with little, like a single parent, aren't shamed for small gifts.

A CEO might give thousands to rebuild a school, a student might tutor kids for free, an unemployed person might give $5 to a shelter—each trusts God to provide. Give from what you have, and God sees the heart. This proportional giving flows from our role as stewards.

3. Giving Is a Matter of Stewardship

We don't own our resources—God does. **"Whoever can be trusted with very little can also be trusted with much..." — Luke 16:10–12**

Picture a single mom stretching her budget to buy groceries for a neighbor, trusting God to provide. That's stewardship—using what you have, rich or poor, for God's glory. The Old Covenant said, "Give 10% and keep the rest." The New Covenant says, "It's all His—use it wisely." Stewardship prepares us to give in ways that cost.

4. Giving Is Sacrificial, Not Safe

Jesus didn't call for easy giving—He called for trust. **"They shared everything they had... so that there were no needy persons among them." — Acts 4:32–35**

The Macedonians gave "beyond their ability" (2 Corinthians 8:3). A college student might give grocery money to a friend. A family might skip dining out to help a single mom. A wealthy couple might delay a project to fund a ministry. Sacrifice stretches faith, no matter your income. When we give until it costs, we're worshiping. This leads us to giving's deeper purpose.

5. Giving Is an Act of Worship

Giving is spiritual, not just financial. Jesus praised the widow's two coins: **"She, out of her poverty, put in everything—all she had to live on." — Mark 12:44**

Her gift was worship, like singing a hymn, saying, "God, You're my treasure." Paul calls gifts a "fragrant offering." **"They are a fragrant of-**

fering, an acceptable sacrifice, pleasing to God." — Philippians 4:18

Whether you're a CEO giving thousands or a retiree volunteering, giving aligns your heart with God's mission. This worship reflects the ultimate Giver.

6. Giving Reflects God's Own Generosity

God's standard is clear: **"For God so loved the world that He gave His one and only Son..."** **— John 3:16**

God gave everything. Our giving—whether money, time, or love—mirrors His heart. It's not about the amount, but the trust we place in Him.

Key Takeaways

- Giving is voluntary, not obligatory (**2 Corinthians 9:7**).

- Give proportionally, not a fixed percentage (**1 Corinthians 16:2**).

- We're stewards, not owners—everything is God's (**Luke 16:10–12**).

- Sacrificial giving reflects trust (**Acts 4:32–35**).

- Giving is worship, honoring God (**Philippians 4:18**).

- We give because God gave everything (**John 3:16**).

Where Do We Go From Here?

If giving is about surrendering everything, are you ready to live with open hands? Many churches still teach tithing, but God calls us to something freer. Let's uncover why tithing persists—and how to embrace the Spirit-led generosity Jesus invites us into. Are you ready to trust Him with everything?

Chapter 6

Living Generously – A Grace-Based Lifestyle

If tithing isn't required, what does faithful giving look like today? How can we live generously without reverting to rules? The answer isn't a percentage—it's a posture. Generosity isn't about checking boxes—it's about faith, surrender, and being ready when God prompts. Let's explore a way of living that says, "Everything I have is God's, and I trust Him to use it through me."

You Don't Own Anything—And That's Good News

Everything you have—money, time, talents—is borrowed. **"The earth is the Lord's, and everything in it." — Psalm 24:1**

You're not an owner—you're a steward. That's freedom, not a burden. You can hold your hands open and say, *"Lord, use what's in them."*

I used to carry extra cash when I traveled—not for me, but for whoever God put in my path. A homeless man needing a meal. A single mom short on rent. A church fundraiser. I wasn't chasing guilt or a campaign—I was listening. When God whispered, *"That person—help them,"* I could act.

Stewardship looks different for everyone: a student volunteering at a shelter, a retiree mentoring youth, a dad fixing a neighbor's car. Whether you're scraping by or secure, it's about using God's gifts for His glory.

Try This: Ask, *"Am I managing my time, money, or skills for God?"* Start small—share a meal, give $5, or offer your skills.

Let the Spirit Lead

How do we know when to give? We ask. We listen. **"Each of you should give what you have decided in your heart to give... for God loves a cheerful giver." — 2 Corinthians 9:7 "If any of you lacks wisdom, you should ask God... and it will be given to you." — James 1:5**

God knows where your gift can make an eternal difference. A friend needing groceries. A missionary raising funds. A neighbor wanting a ride. These are divine appointments. A single parent might give $10 to a church outreach, trusting God for their bills. A professional might sponsor a child's education. The Spirit guides each gift, big or small, because it's about obedience, not obligation.

Try This: Pray daily, *"Lord, who needs what You've given me?"* Act on His nudge—$5, an hour, or a kind word.

Proportional, Not Prescribed

Everyone has something to give—God never asks for what you don't have. **"Each one of you**

should set aside a sum of money in keeping with your income." — 1 Corinthians 16:2

If you're paycheck-to-paycheck, $5 to a food bank is precious. If you're retired, mentoring a teen counts. If you run a business, funding a youth camp reflects your abundance. A widow's $2 can shine brighter than a millionaire's $2,000—it's the faith behind the gift that matters.

Try This: Look at your resources and give joyfully—money, time, or skills. Don't compare; just obey.

Give Like It Costs Something

Jesus saw a widow give her last two coins and said she gave more than the wealthy. **"She, out of her poverty, put in everything—all she had to live on." — Mark 12:44**

God is moved by trust, not comfort. A low-income worker might give $20 to a neighbor, trusting God for their needs. A wealthy donor might fund a community center, adjusting their lifestyle. Sacrifice isn't about dollars—it's about faith.

Try This: Give in a way that makes you pray—donating when money's tight or serving when you're busy.

Support the Church—but Don't Be Bound

Scripture encourages supporting pastors and ministries, but it's love, not law. **"The elders who direct the affairs of the church well are worthy of double honor..." — 1 Timothy 5:17**

Give to your church because God leads you, not because 10% is demanded. A middle-class family might give monthly to outreach. A student might help with Sunday school. A CEO might fund a mission trip. These are acts of worship, like singing a hymn, uniting your heart with God's mission.

Try This: Support your church joyfully, whether with money, time, or service, as the Spirit leads.

Live with Open Hands

Fear whispers, *"What if you give too much?"* Jesus answers: **"Seek first His kingdom... and all these things will be given to you as well." — Matthew 6:33**

This isn't a prosperity scheme—it's a faith promise. A single parent might give $15, trusting God for groceries. A retiree might open their home. Live ready, knowing God will use you.

Try This: Make generosity a rhythm—donate clothes, share a meal, volunteer an hour.

Key Takeaways

- **You're a steward, not an owner—everything is God's.**

- **The Spirit leads giving, not a rulebook.**

- **Give proportionally, not under pressure.**

- **Sacrificial giving is trust, not comfort.**

- **Supporting the church is worship, but voluntary.**

- **Live with open hands, trusting God's provision.**

Where Do We Go From Here?

Now that we know how to live generously, why do churches still teach tithing? Let's uncover this tradition's roots and embrace the freedom of Spirit-led giving. Are you ready to live open-handed?

Chapter 7

Why Tithing Persists—and How to Live Free

If tithing isn't a New Testament command, why do so many churches still teach it? Why does a law-based system linger when Jesus and Paul called us to something freer? The answer lies in history, tradition, and church budgets. But God's vision isn't about percentages—it's about open hands, trust, and love. Let's uncover why tithing persists and how to reclaim the radical generosity Jesus invites us into. Are you ready to live free?

The Early Church Thrived on Love, Not Law

Picture a community where no one clung to possessions, sharing homes, food, and resources because love compelled them to do so.

That's the early church. As we saw in Chapters 2–5, they didn't tithe—they gave:

"Each of you should give what you have decided in your heart..." — 2 Corinthians 9:7 **"They sold property... to give to anyone who had need."** — Acts 2:45 **"...in keeping with your income."** — 1 Corinthians 16:2

For 300 years, Christians gave as the Spirit led. A widow shared her last coins. A merchant funded a missionary. A family opened their home. No percentages—just love in action.

So, when did tithing take over?

How Tithing Became a Church Requirement

Let's step back in time.

The Fourth Century: Constantine's Influence In AD 313, Emperor Constantine legalized Christianity, making it Rome's favored religion. Churches went from house gatherings to owning land and building basilicas. Bishops became civic leaders, and tax exemptions for clergy increased financial needs. To fund this new structure, leaders borrowed the Old Testament tithing model (**Numbers 18:21–24**), turning voluntary gifts into an expectation. It wasn't about worship—it was about keeping the institution running.

The Middle Ages: Tithing as Law By AD 585, European church councils made tithing a legal requirement, backed by fines or jail time. Tithing became a tax to fund cathedrals and clergy, not a heart-led act. Whether you were a poor farmer or a wealthy lord, 10% was demanded, often by force.

The Reformation: A Mixed Legacy In the 1500s, Protestant reformers like Luther challenged Catholic practices, but tithing stuck. Anglicans kept state-enforced tithing, while Baptists often urged 10% as a "biblical standard," blending it with calls to joyful giving (**2 Corinthians 9:7**). This mix of law and grace lingers in many churches today.

Why Modern Churches Cling to Tithing

Today, tithing persists for two reasons:

- **Tradition**: Centuries of teaching have made tithing a Christian norm. Pastors quote **Malachi 3:8–10** ("Will a man rob God?") without its Old Covenant context.

- **Financial Stability**: Churches need funds for salaries, buildings, and ministries. A 10% rule ensures a predictable budget.

Many churches use a hybrid model:

- 10% as a minimum, often with warnings about "robbing God."

- Extra offerings as "cheerful giving."

This creates a two-tiered system, but grace doesn't work in tiers—it flows from trust. The early church thrived without tithing, and modern churches can too:

- A small church might share a pastor's salary, each member giving what they can.

- A community might pool resources for a food pantry—no percentages required.

- A congregation might crowdfund a mission trip, inviting joyful gifts.

There's one more teaching we often miss.

Giving in Secret: Jesus' Radical Call

Jesus taught giving should be humble and hidden:

"When you give to the needy, do not let your left hand know what your right hand is doing, so that your giving may be in secret..." — Matthew 6:3-4

Your hands can't hide from each other—Jesus meant:

- **No show**: He rebuked Pharisees for

flaunting gifts (**Matthew 6:2**). True giving seeks God's eyes, not applause.

- **Second nature**: Giving should flow like breathing, not a calculation.

- **God as audience**: Churches often track giving, but Jesus says, "Let God see."

Contrast with Tithing: Old Testament Tithing: Public, mandatory, measured—New Testament Giving: Private, voluntary, heartfelt.

Picture a single mom slipping $10 into an offering, trusting God for her bills. Or a retiree serving at a shelter, telling no one. These secret acts are worship—free from pride or pressure.

It's Not About the Percentage—It's About the Heart

God doesn't ask for 10%—He asks for your whole heart.

New Testament giving is not:

- A fixed percentage: No 10% rule binds you.

- A church obligation: Giving isn't a fee.

- A prosperity formula: Blessings aren't transactions.

New Testament giving is:

- **Trusting God with everything**: Like the widow's all (**Mark 12:44**).

- **Giving freely and joyfully**: As Paul urged (**2 Corinthians 9:7**).

- **Living with open hands**: Reflecting God's generosity (**John 3:16**).

I met a man who gave half his income to a struggling family, telling only his wife. They prayed, trusting God to provide. That's Jesus' call—not a percentage, but surrender.

Final Challenge: Are You Ready to Live Generously? Your church might teach tithing, and that's okay—supporting God's work is biblical.

But don't let a number define your generosity. Whether you're rich, poor, or in between, God invites you to:

- **Listen to the Spirit**: Pray, "Lord, what do You want me to give today?"

- **Give with trust**: Let $5 or $5,000 stretch your faith.

- **Live open-handed**: Share money, time, or love, knowing God provides.

Jesus didn't raise the bar from 10% to 20%. He raised it to 100%—because in His Kingdom, it's all or nothing.

Are you ready to let go of formulas and live the freedom of Spirit-led generosity?

Chapter 8
More by Christian A. Dickinson

If you enjoyed *It's All or Nothing*, you may also appreciate these Christ-centered resources:

The Unseen Pattern: God's Rhythms in Time, Beauty, and the Gospel

From sunrises to spirals, suffering to celebration, God weaves His redemptive rhythm through creation and Scripture. Christian A. Dickinson, with a mentor's heart and a mathematician's eye, unveils these patterns in stories of loss, hope, and worship, guiding readers to the cross where every moment finds meaning. Blending personal reflection, biblical insight, and invitations to pause, this devotional invites you to notice God's design, trust His grace, and live the harmony of His Gospel.

The Curse of Time: Time Began When Eternity Broke

A theological and personal exploration of time as a consequence of sin—not a neutral part of creation. Drawing from Scripture, Church Fathers, and moments of divine encounter, this book challenges the assumption that time was God's original design and invites readers to rediscover the eternal now of God's presence.

Roar of 'Ēzer: Reclaiming God's Vision for Women's Strength

From Eden's garden to the early church, God named women 'ēzer—rescuer, strength-bearer, equal partner in His image. This compelling biblical exploration invites women to rise, not as shadows but as co-laborers in God's kingdom. With Scripture, story, and a call to courage, *Roar of 'Ēzer* reveals that women were never meant to shrink. They were always meant to roar.

Jesus Was Funnier Than You Think: Unlocking His Wit, Wisdom, and Unexpected Humor

A fresh look at the wit and humor of Jesus Christ — revealing the brilliant, joyful ways He taught truth and disarmed pride.

Every Tear Remembered: God's Presence in Our Grief

A reflection on sorrow, healing, and hope through the lens of God's enduring love.

The Prophetic Equation: Thirty Prophets. One Christ. Zero Coincidence.

An exploration of how thirty prophetic voices across centuries, kingdoms, and crises converge with stunning precision in Jesus Christ — revealing that Scripture is not random, but a masterpiece of divine design.

Micah 6:8: A Prophetic Bridge to Jesus

A concise biblical commentary exploring how one ancient verse points forward to the life and ministry of Christ.

FULL CIRCLE: PREGAME — A Devotional Series for Athletes

Before the whistle blows and the lights come

up, PREGAME challenges athletes to prepare their hearts as well as their bodies. With powerful stories, Scripture reflections, and real talk from the locker room, Coach Dickinson and Anthony "Diso" Paradiso equip competitors to lead with faith, play with integrity, and honor Christ in every moment.

www.ingramcontent.com/pod-product-compliance
Lightning Source LLC
Chambersburg PA
CBHW031257120626
46545CB00007B/2856